DIFFERENT HOURS

DIFFERENT

HOURS

Poems

STEPHEN DUNN

W. W. NORTON & COMPANY
NEW YORK • LONDON

For information about permission to reproduce selections from this book, write to
Permissions, W. W. Norton & Company, Inc.,
500 Fifth Avenue, New York, NY 10110

The text of this book is composed in Fairfield Light
Composition by Sue Carlson
Manufacturing by The Courier Companies, Inc.
Book design by Lovedog Studio

Library of Congress Cataloging-in-Publication Data
Dunn, Stephen, date.
Different hours : poems / Stephen Dunn.
p.   cm.
ISBN 0-393-04986-8
I. Title.

PS3554.U49 D54 2000
811'.54—dc21   00-030556

W. W. Norton & Company, Inc., 500 Fifth Avenue, New York, N.Y. 10110
www.wwnorton.com

W. W. Norton & Company Ltd., 10 Coptic Street, London WC1A 1PU

2 3 4 5 6 7 8 9 0

CONTENTS

ACKNOWLEDGMENTS

The Alaska Quarterly: "After"

APR: "The Death of God," "Men in the Sky," "Oklahoma City"

Barrow Street: "A Spiritual Woman," "Another Man"

The Georgia Review: "What Goes On," "A Postmortem Guide," "At the Restaurant," "Art," "Rubbing," Returning from an Artist's Studio," "The Overt," "Phantom," "Sixty," "The Reverse Side," "His Town," "The Party," "Losing Steps," "Zero Hour"

Green Mountains Review: "Story"

The Kenyon Review: "Before the Sky Darkens," "The Sexual Revolution"

Michigan Quarterly Review: "Their Divorce"

The New Republic: "Irresistible," "Visiting the Master"

The New Yorker: "Empathy"

Ploughshares: "Evanescence," "John & Mary," "So Far"

Poetry: "The Metaphysicians of South Jersey," "Old Dogs," "Androgyne," "Emperors," "Chokecherry"

Prairie Schooner: "Different Hours," "Nature," "Simpler Times," "Our Parents"

The Southern Review: "Backwaters," "Capriccio Italien," "Dog Weather," "Odysseus's Secret," "Optimism," "One Moment and the Next in the Pine Barrens," "The Last Hours," "The Same Cold"

Thanks to my loyal and scrupulous readers Lawrence Raab, Philip Booth, Carol Houck Smith, Greg Djanikian, and my wife, Lois. And for important residencies at The MacDowell Colony and Yaddo, as well as a grant from Richard Stockton College.

What is eloquent is the passing moment
and the moment that will come after it.

—Maurice Blanchot

I only regret my economies.

—Reynolds Price

I

BEFORE THE SKY DARKENS

Sunsets, incipient storms, the tableaus
of melancholy—maybe these are
the Saturday night-events
to take your best girl to. At least then
there might be moments of vanishing beauty
before the sky darkens,
and the expectation of happiness
would hardly exist
and therefore might be possible.

More and more you learn to live
with the unacceptable.
You sense the ever-hidden God
retreating even farther,
terrified or embarrassed.
You might as well be a clown,
big silly clothes, no evidence of desire.

That's how you feel, say, on a Tuesday.
Then out of the daily wreckage
comes an invitation
with your name on it. Or more likely,
that best girl of yours offers you,
once again, a small local kindness.

You open your windows to good air
blowing in from who knows where,
which you gulp and deeply inhale
as if you have a death sentence. You have.
All your life, it seems, you've been appealing it.
Night sweats and useless strategem. Reprieves.

SIXTY

Because in my family the heart goes first
and hardly anybody makes it out of his fifties,
I think I'll stay up late with a few bandits
of my choice and resist good advice.
I'll invent a secret scroll lost by Egyptians
and reveal its contents: the directions
to your house, recipes for forgiveness.
History says my ventricles are stone alleys,
my heart itself a city with a terrorist
holed up in the mayor's office.
I'm in the mood to punctuate
only with that maker of promises, the colon:
next, next, next, its says, God bless it.
As García Lorca may have written: some people
forget to live as if a great arsenic lobster
could fall on their heads at any moment.
My sixtieth birthday is tomorrow.
Come, play poker with me,
I want to be taken to the cleaners.
I've had it with all stingy-hearted sons of bitches.
A heart is to be spent. As for me, I'll share
my mulcher with anyone who needs to mulch.

It's time to give up the search for the invisible.
On the best of days there's little more
than the faintest intimations. The millennium,
my dear, is sure to disappoint us.
I think I'll keep on describing things
to ensure that they really happened.

EVANESCENCE

The silhouette of a mountain. Above it
a dark halo of rain. Dusk's light
fading, holding on. He thinks he's seen
some visible trace of some absent thing.
Knows he won't talk about it, can't.
He arrives home to the small winter pleasures
of a clothes tree, a hatrack,
his heroine in a housedress saying hello.
He could be anyone aware of an almost,
not necessarily sad. He could be a brute
suddenly chastened by the physical world.
They talk about the storm in the mountains
destined for the lowlands, the béarnaise sauce
and the fine cut of beef it improves.
The commonplace and its contingincies,
his half-filled cup, the monstrous
domesticated by the six o'clock news—
these are his endurances,
in fact his *privileges,* if he has any sense.
Later while they make love, he thinks of
Mantle's long home run in the '57 Series.
He falls to sleep searching for a word.

At the Restaurant

Life would be unbearable
if we made ourselves conscious of it.
— Fernando Pessoa

Six people are too many people
and a public place the wrong place
for what you're thinking—

stop this now.

Who do you think you are?
The duck à l'orange is spectacular,
the flan the best in town.

But there among your friends
is the unspoken, as ever,
chatter and gaiety its familiar song.

And there's your chronic emptiness
spiraling upward in search of words
you'll dare not say

without irony.
You should have stayed at home.
It's part of the social contract

to seem to be where your body is,
and you've been elsewhere like this,
for Christ's sake, countless times;

behave, feign.

Certainly you believe a part of decency
is to overlook, to let pass?
Praise the Caesar salad. Praise Susan's

black dress, Paul's promotion and raise.
Inexcusable, the slaughter in this world.
Insufficient, the merely decent man.

THE DEATH OF GOD

When the news filtered to the angels
they were overwhelmed by their sudden aloneness.
Long into the night they waited for instructions;
the night was quieter than any night they'd known.
I don't have a thought in my head, one angel lamented.
Others worried, Is there such a thing as an angel now?
New to questioning, dashed by the dry light
of reason, some fell into despair. Many disappeared.
A few wandered naturally toward power, were hired
by dictators who needed something like an angel
to represent them to the world.
These angels spoke the pure secular word.
They murdered sweetly and extolled the greater good.
The Dark Angel himself was simply amused.

The void grew, and was fabulously filled.
Vast stadiums and elaborate malls—
the new cathedrals—were built
where people cheered and consumed.
At the nostalgia shops angel trinkets
and plastic crucifixes lined the shelves.
The old churches were homes for the poor.

And yet before meals and at bedtime
and in the iconographies of dreams,
God took his invisible place in the kingdom of need.
Disaffected minstrels made and sang His songs.
The angels were given breath and brain.
This all went on while He was dead to the world.

The Dark Angel observed it, waiting as ever.
On these things his entire existence depended.

CAPRICCIO ITALIEN

From the mountain drifts down the finest mist,
so fine you walk in it, letting it glaze
your hair, while boats on the lake bob and blur.
This is not your country; everything you see—
cobblestoned ancient streets, umbrella'd tables,
laundry hanging from the balconies of the poor—
appears meaningful.
Just off the piazza, a window display
of squab and rabbit and roasted pig.
No outsized dream sullens the friendly clerks.
If they're unhappy you're happy
a tradition helps them not to let it show.
You buy the most expensive tie you've ever bought,
silk and wide, blue with subtle, well-spaced dots.
You try on a flamboyant scarf. In the mirror
someone foolish stares back at you.
You take it anyhow.
You're a woman's man, and you're womanless.
How absurd to think anyone can escape
being judged for what he doesn't have.
Oh the chosen gloomy beauty of a tourist town—
you've always known
what lifts you up can get you down.
You've come far to feel this keenly low.
The pigeons coo their greedy songs.

You break off bits of bread and leave no trail.
At dusk, if the mist is gone, you plan to sit
with some grappa in a slender glass.
You're sure the swallows won't disappoint—
swoop and dive as they did the night before,
mindless, wild, wholly in control.

OLD DOGS

Those Trotskys of relationships,
perpetual revolution their motto,
their impatient hearts
dangerous to all that's complacent,

I understand them perfectly
and also why someone they've left behind
might travel all the way to Mexico
with a pickaxe to put an end to things.

It's human nature, after all, to want
to put an end to things.

And to start up again.

"Because you can't teach old dogs new tricks,"
Dinah Washington said,
"you got to get yourself some new dogs."
She was explaining her eight husbands,
and this was an argument for nine.

If I'd known any one of her old dogs
no doubt I'd understand why he might
have wanted just to lie on the couch
and go for short walks.

I've wanted to do nothing
as often as I've wanted to rise up,
rush into the night.

Falling in love produces such anxiety,
my friend says, thank God there's sex
for some occasional repose.
He lives for scattered episodes
with one woman at a time.

I understand that, too,

as I understand year after year
doing a few same things
in the same house with the same person,
settled and unsettled, in for the long haul.

ODYSSEUS'S SECRET

At first he thought only of home, and Penelope.
But after a few years, like anyone on his own,
he couldn't separate what he'd chosen
from what had chosen him. Calypso,
                        the Lotus-eaters, Circe;
a man could forget where he lived.
He had a gift for getting in and out of trouble,
a prodigious, human gift. To survive Cyclops
and withstand the Sirens' song—
just those words *survive, withstand,*
                        in his mind became a music
he moved to and lived by.
How could *govern*, even *love*, compete?
They belonged to a different part of a man,
the untested part, which never had transcended dread,
or the liar part, which always spoke like a citizen.
                        The larger the man, though,
the more he needed to be reminded
he was a man. Lightning, high winds;
for every excess a punishment.
Penelope *was* dear to him,
                        full of character and fine in bed.
But by the middle years this other life
had become his life. That was Odysseus's secret,
kept even from himself. When he talked about return

he thought he meant what he said.

                Twenty years to get home?

A man finds his shipwrecks,

tells himself the necessary stories.

Whatever gods are—our own fearful voices

or intimations from the unseen order

of things, the gods finally released him,

                cleared the way.

Odysseus boarded that Phaeacian ship, suddenly tired

of the road's dangerous enchantments,

and sailed through storm and wild sea

as if his beloved were all that ever mattered.

WHAT GOES ON

After the affair and the moving out,
after the destructive revivifying passion,
we watched her life quiet

into a new one, her lover more and more
on its periphery. She spent many nights
alone, happy for the narcosis

of the television. When she got cancer
she kept it to herself until she couldn't
keep it from anyone. The chemo debilitated
and saved her, and one day

her husband asked her to come back—
his wife, who after all had only fallen
in love as anyone might
who hadn't been in love in a while—

and he held her, so different now,
so thin, her hair just partially
grown back. He held her like a new woman

and what she felt
felt almost as good as love had,
and each of them called it love
because precision didn't matter anymore.

And we who'd been part of it,
often rejoicing with one
and consoling the other,

we who had seen her truly alive
and then merely alive,
what could we do but revise
our phone book, our hearts,

offer a little toast to what goes on.

THEIR DIVORCE

Not them. Not even with the best
binoculars on the bluest day
could I have seen it coming.
Not with scrutiny's microscope,
or with the help of history or gossip.
Of all people, not them.
They hadn't fallen in love with others.
Not even a night of drink
or proximity's slow burn drove them
to lapse, say, with a coworker.
It means no one can know what goes on
in the pale trappings of bedrooms,
in anyone's secret, harrowed heart.
It makes time itself an executioner—
a fact I always knew
applied to couples
whose bodies contradicted
their Darling this, Honey that,
and even some who exhibited
true decency and respect.
But this is a mockery, a defeat.
My friends were perfect, *perfect*.

"Every married couple appearing together
in public is comic," Adorno said,
and I wrote "Stupid!" in the margin.
Now they're broken up, finished.
Oh Adorno, you son of a bitch,
you perspicacious bastard,
sometimes what a cold eye sees
lasts longer than any of us.

DOG WEATHER

Earlier, everyone was in knee boots, collars up.
The paper boy's papers came apart
in the wind.

Now, nothing human moving.
Just a black squirrel fidgeting like Bogart
in *The Caine Mutiny*.

My breath chalks the window,
gives me away to myself.

I like the intelligibility of old songs.
I prefer yesterday.

Cars pass, the asphalt's on its back
smudged with skid. It's potholed
and cracked; it's no damn good.

Anyone out without the excuse of a dog
should be handcuffed
and searched for loneliness.

My hair is thinning.
I feel like tossing the wind a stick.

The promised snow has arrived,
heavy, wet.
I remember the blizzard of . . .
People I don't want to be
speak like that.

I close my eyes and one
of my many unborn sons
makes a snowball
and lofts it at an unborn friend.

They've sent me an AARP card.
I'm on their list.

I can be discounted now almost anywhere.

OPTIMISM

My friend the pessimist thinks I'm optimistic
because I seem to believe in the next good thing.
But I see rueful shadows almost everywhere.
When the sun rises I think of collisions and AK-47s.
It's my mother's fault, who praised and loved me,
sent me into the dreadful world as if
it would tell me a story I'd understand. The fact is
optimism is the enemy of happiness.
I've learned to live for the next good thing
because lifelong friends write good-bye letters,
because regret follows every timidity.
I'm glad I know that all great romances are fleshed
with failure. I'll take a day of bitterness and rain
to placate the gods, to get it over with.
My mother told me I could be a great pianist
because I had long fingers. My fingers are small.
It's my mother's fault, every undeserved sweetness.

ANDROGYNE

My lost love, back when Zeus split us in two—
our intelligence and completeness
a threat to the gods—this ache
began, this perpetual wandering . . .

I've seen you in the teeming, concupiscent
streets, I married you, at dusk I followed you
into bars; every time I found you
I recognized you as someone seen before.
I could not choose not to respond to desire.
Only you understand.

Old now, I admit to you
I've been content for hours watching deer
play out their nimble, nervous lives.
I've considered flowers and without sadness
watched them drop their yellow leaves.

In dreams you still whisper to me
and in dreams I whisper back.
But we make fewer plans.

I will tell you, Androgyne, what I learned today
about the sublime. It's that moment
when a compound changes
from one state to another. It's chemistry.
All lovers know it's chemistry,
not physics, that makes the world go round.

And maybe when we meet again
after one of our long journeys toward the other,
you will find me wishing
to do little more than brush back
a lock of hair that's fallen
across your face, too close to an eye.

We'll be sitting side by side,
noontime, in a park.
We'll not be able to see the sun
due to the excess of light.
I'll raise my hand to your face
and you'll tilt your cheek my way,
and I'll move that lock of hair, now gray,
to where I've always liked it to be.

ZERO HOUR

It was the hour of simply nothing,
not a single desire in my western heart,
and no ancient system
of breathing and postures,
no big idea justifying what I felt.

There was even an absence of despair.

"Anything goes," I said to myself.
All the clocks were high. Above them,
hundreds of stars flicking *if, if, if*.
Everywhere in the universe, it seemed,
some next thing was gathering itself.

I started to feel something,
but it was nothing more than a moment
passing into another, or was it less
eloquent than that, purely muscular,
some meaningless twitch?

I'd let someone else make it rhyme.

THE HOURS

Worst was to live by somebody else's time,
the hours scheduled for him, smudged
with clarity and motives not his own.

He preferred the enigmas of early morning

and the neither-here-nor-thereness of dusk,
which gave the half-life he lived an atmosphere.
He liked watching it collect itself,
impossible to tell if it descended or rose.

He didn't care for noon's bustle and blare.
And evenings couldn't be trusted, he felt,
so dependent were they on other people.

Even evenings alone were measured
by who wasn't there. Desire & Need,
how they sat down with him,
helped like untrained helpers
arrange the hours that followed.
Evening was their time.

He remembered, of course, the lovely hours—
the body's sudden holidays, prolonged fiestas
of the mind. He rewound and rewound.

II

THE PARTY

After I buried the century's putrid corpse
and resolved to rid the world
of utopias and the fat
which had collected around my waist,

I kissed the lovely one I was with
and a few others I might as easily have slugged.
How festive it was at the mausoleum!
Even I wanted to dance the tarantella

until dawn, make love shamelessly in the open.
A few enemies extended their hands
and when the famous sentimentalist spoke
about his inner weather my heart sank so low

I poured myself a large, neat glass of Glenfiddich.
"Houston," I said, "Tranquility Base here,
the Eagle has landed." And my best friend laughed.
Meanwhile, the century had begun to stir

in its coffin; several of us sensed it.
Maybe it was the best parts of it
twitching to be remembered? Maybe Churchill
and Kafka and a handful of edgy others

were appalled by the stench so near them?
But by this time all of us were used
to injustice. We partied on
into the *tabula rasa* of the new century

as if somehow we could erase our pasts
by just moving forward,
as if, come morning, we wouldn't wake
with the bitterest nostalgias.

SIMPLER TIMES

The violent boys merely armed
with fists, the president
avuncular, his office unspoiled,

it's tempting to believe
we lived in simpler times.

Unfulfillment didn't have
its high priests, not even a language.
I just thought of it as family life

or school, and on Sunday nights
ran in from the clean, safe streets
to laugh at Milton Berle.

I wanted to be a regular guy,
she a popular girl.
That night she baby-sat, oh

a breast never again would be
that sufficient or that bare.
I stopped right there.

Nearby were the slums
just beyond our caring,
and nearer still—it took years

to hear it—a complaint
rising to a howl.
In Hungary the tanks

rolled in. In Zaire
Mobutu filled the secret,
underground jails.

OUR PARENTS

For my brother

Our parents died at least twice,
the second time when we forgot their stories,
or couldn't imagine how often they craved love,
or felt useless, or yearned for some justice
in this world. In their graves, our parents' need
for us is pure, they're lost without us.
Their honeymoon in Havana does or does not
exist. That late August in the Catskills—
we can decide to make them happy.

What is the past if not unfinished work,
swampy, fecund, seductively revisable?
One of us has spent his life developing respect
for the weakness of words, the other for what
must be held on to; there may be a chance for us.

We try to say what happened in that first house
where we were, like most children, the only
needy people on earth. We remember
what we were forbidden, who got the biggest slice.
Our parents, meanwhile, must have wanted something
back from us. We know what it is, don't we?
We've been alive long enough.

EMPATHY

Once in a small rented room, awaiting
a night call from a distant time zone,
I understood you could feel so futureless
you'd want to get a mermaid

tattooed on your biceps. Company
forever. Flex and she'd dance.
The phone never rang, except for those
phantom rings, which I almost answered.

I was in D.C., on leave from the army.
It was a woman, of course, who didn't call.
Or, as we said back then, a girl.
It's anybody's story.

But I think for me it was the beginning
of empathy, not a large empathy
like the deeply selfless might have,
more like a leaning, like being able

to imagine a life for a spider, a maker's
life, or just some aliveness
in its wide abdomen and delicate spinnerets
so you take it outside in two paper cups

instead of stepping on it.
The next day she called, and it was final.
I remember going to the zoo
and staring a long time

at the hippopotamus, its enormous weight
and mass, its strange appearance
of tranquility.
And then the sleek, indignant cats.

Then I went back to Fort Jackson.
I had a calendar taped inside my locker,
and I'd circle days for which I
had no plans, not even hopes—

big circles, so someone might ask.
It was between wars. Only the sergeants
and a few rawboned farm boys
took learning how to kill seriously.

We had to traverse the horizontal ladder,
rung after rung, to pass
into mess hall. Always the weak-handed,
the weak-armed, couldn't make it.

I looked for those who didn't laugh
at those of us who fell.
In the barracks, after drills,
the quiet fellowship of the fallen.

THE LAST HOURS

There's some innocence left,
and these are the last hours of an empty afternoon
at the office, and there's the clock
on the wall, and my friend Frank
in the adjacent cubicle selling himself
on the phone.
                    I'm twenty-five, on the shaky
ladder up, my father's son, corporate,
clean-shaven, and I know only what I don't want,
which is almost everything I have.
                    A meeting ends.
Men in serious suits, intelligent men
who've been thinking hard about marketing snacks,
move back now to their window offices, worried
or proud. The big boss, Horace,
had called them in to approve this, reject that—
the big boss, a first-name, how's-your-family
kind of assassin, who likes me.
                    It's 1964.
The sixties haven't begun yet. Cuba is a larger name
than Vietnam. The Soviets are behind
everything that could be wrong. Where I sit
it's exactly nineteen minutes to five. My phone rings.
Horace would like me to stop in

before I leave. *Stop in.* Code words,
leisurely words, that mean *now.*
                    Would I be willing
to take on this? Would X's office, who by the way
is no longer with us, be satisfactory?
About money, will this be enough?
I smile, I say yes and yes and yes,
but—I don't know from what calm place
this comes—I'm translating
his beneficence into a lifetime, a life
of selling snacks, talking snack strategy,
thinking snack thoughts.
                    On the elevator down
it's a small knot, I'd like to say, of joy.
That's how I tell it now, here in the future,
the fear long gone.
By the time I reach the subway it's grown,
it's outsized, an attitude finally come round,
and I say it quietly to myself, *I quit,*
and keep saying it, knowing I will say it, sure
of nothing else but.

LUCK

1

After I set the corner lot on fire
not even God saw me hiding
between the garages.
My mother said the boy
can do no wrong.
My father told everyone:
This is my son.
Years passed.
The ball took a bad hop
and I was safe.
Anita Bolby invited me in.

2

The Gauchos cornered me
behind the 7-Eleven;
a broken finger, bloody nose.
Something attacked my father's heart.
The horse in the fifth
couldn't lose.
My crucial shot rolled round
the rim, then out.

No one, suddenly, cared.
Madeline White said No,
not here or anywhere.

   3

At the gaming tables I felt it
move to the dealer
and back to me.
How often, I heard it threaten,
do you wish to be a fool?
By this time
I had a wife and children
and a house on spectacular loan.
Here's what I believed:
I knew how not to love it
more than it would allow.

THE SEXUAL REVOLUTION

In that time of great freedom to touch
   and get in touch,
we lived on the prairie amid polite

moral certainty. The sensate world seemed
   elsewhere, and was.
On our color television the president's body

admitted he was lying. There was marching
   in the suddenly charged streets,
and what a girl in a headband and miniskirt

called *communication*. A faraway friend wrote
   to say the erotic life
was the only life. Get with it, he said.

But many must have been slow-witted
   during The Age of Enlightenment,
led artless lives during The Golden Age.

We watched the revolution on the evening news.
   It was 1972
when the sixties reached all the way

to where we were. The air became alive
　　with incense and license.
The stores sold permission and I bought

and my wife bought until we were left
　　with almost nothing.
Even the prairie itself changed;

people began to call it the Land, and once again
　　it was impossibly green
and stretched endlessly ahead of us.

THE SAME COLD

In Minnesota the serious cold arrived
like no cold I'd previously experienced,
an in-your-face honesty to it, a clarity
that always took me by surprise.
On blizzardy nights with wires down
or in the dead-battery dawn
the cold made good neighbors of us all,
made us moral because we might need
something moral in return, no hitchhiker
left on the road, not even some frozen
strange-looking stranger turned away
from our door. After a spell of it,
I remember, zero would feel warm—
people out for walks, jackets open,
ice fishermen in the glory
of their shacks moved to Nordic song.
The cold took over our lives,
lived in every conversation, as compelling
as local dirt or local sport.
If bitten by it, stranded somewhere,
a person would want
to lie right down in it and sleep.
Come February, some of us needed
to scream, hurt ourselves, divorce.

Once, on Route 23, thirty below,
my Maverick seized up, and a man
with a blanket and a candy bar, a man
for all weather, stopped and drove me home.
It was no big thing to him, the savior.
Just two men, he said, in the same cold.

LOSING STEPS

1

It's probably a Sunday morning
in a pickup game, and it's clear
you've begun to leave
fewer people behind.

Your fakes are as good as ever,
but when you move
you're like the Southern Pacific
the first time a car kept up with it,

your opponent at your hip,
with you all the way
to the rim. Five years earlier
he'd have been part of the air

that stayed behind you
in your ascendance.
On the sidelines they're saying,
He's lost a step.

2

In a few more years
it's adult night in a gymnasium
streaked with the abrupt scuff marks
of high schoolers, and another step

leaves you like a wire
burned out in a radio.
You're playing defense,
someone jukes right, goes left,

and you're not fooled
but he's past you anyway,
dust in your eyes,
a few more points against you.

3

Suddenly you're fifty;
if you know anything about steps
you're playing chess
with an old, complicated friend.

But you're walking to a schoolyard
where kids are playing full-court,
telling yourself
the value of experience, a worn down

basketball under your arm,
your legs hanging from your waist
like misplaced sloths in a country
known for its cheetahs and its sunsets.

AFTER

Jack and Jill at home together after their fall,
the bucket spilled, her knees badly scraped,
and Jack with not even an aspirin for what's broken.
We can see the arduous evenings ahead of them.
And the need now to pay a boy to fetch the water.
Our mistake was trying to do something together,
Jill sighs. Jack says, If you'd have let go for once
you wouldn't have come tumbling after.
He's in a wheelchair, but she's still an item—
for the rest of their existence confined
to a little, rhyming story. We tell it to our children,
who laugh, already accustomed to disaster.
We'd like to teach them the secrets
of knowing how to go too far,
but Jack is banging with his soup spoon,
Jill is pulling out her hair. Out of decency
we turn away, as if it were possible to escape
the drift of our lives, the fundamental business
of making do with what's been left us.

So Far

A wild incipience in the air
as if everything stilled
is deeply active, the night cascading
through the tall pines
until it's in the house.
I don't feel just yet
like turning on the lights.
There's an unlikable bird
chuckling outside the window.
Another bird says to it
tsk, tsk.
The end of summer is upon us.
Our kids are grown,
have entered the venal world
with some of the equipment
it takes to survive.
So far so good.
McVeigh's been found guilty.
My wife's in California, visiting
friends she once was young with
who can always make her laugh.
I've never been the kind
who feels deathly in autumn.
I don't bring home the landscape.

But more and more
it just comes in, presses down,
finds correlatives in me.
The moon's shining now
through the big window.
In the world I can't help
but live in, it seems
the cold and the righteous
are no less dangerous
than the furious, the crazed.
Everywhere, an error
leading to an error.
Everywhere the justified.

DIFFERENT HOURS

As the small plane descended through
the it's-all-over-now Sturm und Drang
I closed my eyes and saw myself
in waves of lucidity, a vanisher
in a long process of vanishing,
of solitary character, truant heart.
When we landed, I flipped down
my daily mask, resumed my normal
dreamy life of uncommitted crimes.
I held nothing against me anymore.
And now, next day, I wake before
the sound of traffic, amazed
that the paper has been delivered,
that the world is up and working.
A dazed rabbit sits in the dewy grass.
The clematis has no aspirations
as it climbs its trestle.
I pour myself orange juice, Homestyle.
I say the hell with low-fat cream cheese,
and slather the good stuff on my bagel.
The newspaper seems to be thinking
my thoughts: No Hope for Lost Men.
Link Between Laughter and Health.
It says scientists now know the neutrino

has mass. "The most ghostly particle
in the universe," one of them called it.
No doubt other scientists are jealous
who asked the right questions
too late, some small failure of intuition
leading them astray.
No doubt, too, at this very moment
a snake is sunning itself in Calcutta.
And somewhere a philosopher is erasing
"time's empty passing" because he's seen
a woman in a ravishing dress.
In a different hour he'll put it back.

III

THE REVERSE SIDE

The reverse side also has a reverse side.

—A JAPANESE PROVERB

It's why when we speak a truth
some of us instantly feel foolish
as if a deck inside us has been shuffled
and there it is—the opposite
of what we said.

And perhaps why as we fall in love
we're already falling out of it.

It's why the terrified and the simple
latch onto one story,
just one version of the great mystery.

Image & afterimage, oh even
the open-minded yearn for a fiction
to rein things in—
the snapshot, the lie of a frame.

How do we not go crazy,
we who have found ourselves compelled
to live with the circle, the ellipsis, the word
not yet written.

THE OVERT

For the reader

The town idiot who walked the streets
with a beatific smile
must have been bewildered
by our stones, back then
when I was a child.

It's an act of will and confession
to bring him forward now,
my first gesture to you.

To hide myself from myself
I've used various veils of weather,
the hopeful smell of just-cut grass.
"What a nice day to be alive," I've said,

while headlines screamed atrocity
and I couldn't locate what I felt.

The street violinist who played for me
in her evening dress
simultaneously lived with Bach

and the clang of my coins.
Nearby, a juggler succeeded
in keeping three things alive.

What could be more normal
than a double, even a triple life?

Still, I remember being surprised
by the ineffectual shy biologist
at his retirement party,
how well he spoke,
how, even with his wife,
he fast-danced all night long.

"Though the events and dates
may remain at odds,"
I said to my host
as we walked the Ponte Vecchio,
"I'd like you to believe everything I say."

Is the life we lead in public
obscene?
Would you say that what I've offered here
is overt?

You must worry about trusting a man
who feels he's damned
and knows there's a certain charm
in admitting it.

JOHN & MARY

John & Mary had never met. They were like
two hummingbirds who also had never met.
—FROM A FRESHMAN'S SHORT STORY

They were like gazelles who occupied different
grassy plains, running in opposite directions
from different lions. They were like postal clerks
in different zip codes, with different vacation time,
their bosses adamant and clock-driven.
How could they get together?
They were like two people who couldn't get together.
John was a Sufi with a love of the dervish,
Mary of course a Christian with a curfew.
They were like two dolphins in the immensity
of the Atlantic, one playful,
the other stuck in a tuna net—
two absolutely different childhoods!
There was simply no hope for them.
They would never speak in person.
When they ran across that windswept field
toward each other, they were like two freight trains,

one having left Seattle at 6:36 P.M.
at an unknown speed, the other delayed
in Topeka for repairs.
The math indicated that they'd embrace
in another world, if at all, like parallel lines.
Or merely appear kindred and close, like stars.

ART

"Vissi d'arte," sang Callas on my boombox
and, alone in early evening, swept up and stilled,
I saw myself as husband, poet, slackard,
undriven drifter through house and world.
I knew I could be distracted by weather,
lured by box scores and décolletage.
Puccini, though, must have lived for art,
as Callas certainly did, which is no doubt why
a small tear formed in the corner
of my left eye, a kind of applause.
At which the mood-insensitive clock gestured
my wife's plane would soon touch down.
I didn't want to move. Was Puccini
ever taken from such a fine moment?
Was Callas? They must have been, of course.
And couldn't bear it. Or ranted anyway
because they were brilliantly selfish,
or what involved them just then
was magical, in a sense their lives,
a virtuosity that shouldn't be disturbed.
Outside, the wind chime began to chime.
I was sure the promised storm would flirt,
then veer north. I had to stop
for gas. I had to make the bed I hadn't made

since she left. Was the indoor cat in?
Were the windows down? All the way
to the airport I tried to time amber,
beat red. I parked in short term. I ran.
Man of urgency. Man of what later,
with feeling, might be sung.

RUBBING

"Anything that you rub long enough becomes beautiful."

—JIM OPINSKY

I once saw a painter smear black paint
on a bad blue sky,
then rub it in until that lie of hers

was gone. I've seen men polish cars
so hard they've given off light.
As a child I kept a stone in my pocket,

thumb and forefinger in collusion
with water and wind,
caressing it day and night.

I've begun a few things with an eraser,
waited for friction's spark.
I've learned that sometimes severe

can lead to truer, even true.
But few things human can stand
to be rubbed for long—I know this

and can't stop. If beauty comes
it comes startled, hiding scars,
out of what barely can be endured.

A SPIRITUAL WOMAN

After Joyce Tenneson's photograph
"Body and Fabric"

It's as if she's praying, hands palm-to-palm,
a transparent gauzy fabric draping her,
revealing her breasts, and from her shoulders
two gossamer strips extending downward
in a gorgeous hint of wings. Those praying hands
point to, are almost in place of, the place
between her legs. If her body is making
an invitation it's clearly inward, to itself.
It would be disastrous to want her.
Her neck is visible, but not her face—
a placid mountain tarn, I imagine—
unreachable except by snowshoes and guts.
A woman who holds herself like this
is more nude than she will ever be naked.
It would be good to be in her presence
after having made love to someone else,
my cock unworried and small and happy
to be asleep. I'd ask what she's been reading,
what she does for fun, I'd wonder
if she might have something to teach me
about patience and the void

I'm always trying to fill. Wouldn't it then
be time to try to make her laugh, laughter
one sure ticket to where the spiritual is?
Or would she have gone further inward,
away from my annoying speculations
and stare, thinking to herself (wrongly),
"No man will ever follow me there."

IRRESISTIBLE

After the film UN COEUR EN HIVER

No one ever has heard her subtleties
or mistakes as keenly,
has heard her the way
she most deeply hears herself,

so the brilliant, beautiful violinist
gives up her husband for the artisan
who repairs her violin. Character
on its way toward destiny—

my favorite kind of helplessness.
She loves his cold, uncompromising ear.
But he loves only music and violins
and small adjustments;

he doesn't desire her, or anyone.
What she sees as affection
he means as good work,
and the winter in his heart

must seem to her a climate
only she can improve. She persists—
a fool, an idiot, my intimate—
and the film slows

to him listening at a concert.
He smiles at Ravel played just right.
Afterward he isolates for her the precise
moment. It's what she can't resist.

He works for her husband,
but this fact has nothing to do
with why he turns her away.
That would have been understandable

and simply moral, and I wouldn't
have walked out into the welter
of the night, into the fraught air,
so happily implicated and encumbered.

Returning from an Artist's Studio

Late at night in my one life
I see fireflies scintillating a field
and a fullish moon up there working
on its reputation, which I thought
was secure. And though I'm not one
to stop my car for beauty
I stop, get out, begin to understand
how the first stories winked
of another world. It's as if
I'm witness to some quiet carnival
of the gods, or the unrisen dead
speaking in code.

Insects are eating each other. Stunned
beyond fear, mice are being given
their first and last flights,
talons holding them dear.
The fox has found a warren.
Everything I can't see
is at least as real as what I can.
If I stand here long enough
I'll hear a bark and a squeal.

The artist had an eye for exaggerated sunsets
splashed with rain, odd collisions
of roots, animals, seeds.
I didn't like a thing I saw,
so much effort to be strange.
The moon is hanging from a leafy branch.
The fireflies are libidinous
and will not be denied.

STORY

A woman's taking her late-afternoon walk
on Chestnut where no sidewalk exists
and houses with gravel driveways
sit back among the pines. Only the house
with the vicious dog is close to the road.
An electric fence keeps him in check.
When she comes to that house, the woman
always crosses to the other side.

I'm the woman's husband. It's a problem
loving your protagonist too much.
Soon the dog is going to break through
that fence, teeth bared, and go for my wife.
She will be helpless. I'm out of town,
helpless too. Here comes the dog.
What kind of dog? A mad dog, a dog
like one of those teenagers who just loses it
on the playground, kills a teacher.

Something's going to happen that can't happen
in a good story: out of nowhere a car
comes and kills the dog. The dog flies
in the air, lands in a patch of delphiniums.
My wife is crying now. The woman who hit

the dog has gotten out of her car. She holds
both hands to her face. The woman who owns
the dog has run out of her house. Three women
crying in the street, each for different reasons.

All of this is so unlikely; it's as if
I've found myself in a country of pure fact,
miles from truth's more demanding realm.
When I listened to my wife's story on the phone
I knew I'd take it from her, tell it
every which way until it had an order
and a deceptive period at the end. That's what
I always do in the face of helplessness,
make some arrangements if I can.

Praise the odd, serendipitous world.
Nothing I'd be inclined to think of
would have stopped that dog.
Only the facts saved her.

VISITING THE MASTER

Don't follow me, I'm lost,
the master said to the follower
who had a cocked pen
and a yellow pad.

But I live for art, the follower said.
I need to know some of its secrets,
if not its rules.

I'm lost, said the master,
I ask only for your forbearance
and a little help with the rent.

The follower realized he'd caught
the master at a bad time.
I'll come back next week, he said.

He knew the master had told others
that over a lifetime
the word *autumn* shouldn't be used
more than five or six times,
and that only a fool
confuses activity with energy.

The follower came back the next week.

The master said, go away.
It all begins elsewhere, apart from me.
Both sunshine and shadow, these days,
oppress me. A good woman
is hard to keep.

The follower thought he understood.
You mean, he said, privation
is the key?

Oh, return to zero, the master said.
Use what's lying around the house.
Make it simple and sad.

IV

THE METAPHYSICIANS
OF SOUTH JERSEY

Because in large cities the famous truths
already had been plumbed and debated,
the metaphysicians of South Jersey lowered
their gaze, just tried to be themselves.
They'd gather at coffee shops in Vineland
and deserted shacks deep in the Pine Barrens.
Nothing they came up with mattered
so they were free to be eclectic, and as odd
as getting to the heart of things demanded.
They walked undisguised on the boardwalk.
At the Hamilton Mall they blended
with the bargain-hunters and the feckless.
Almost everything amazed them,
the last hour of a county fair,
blueberry fields covered with mist.
They sought the approximate weight of sadness,
its measure and coloration. But they liked
a good ball game too, well pitched, lots of zeroes
on the scoreboard. At night when they lay down,
exhausted and enthralled, their spouses knew

it was too soon to ask any hard questions.
Come breakfast, as always, the metaphysicians
would begin to list the many small things
they'd observed and thought, unable to stop talking
about this place and what a world it was.

HIS TOWN

The town was in the mists of chaos.

—A STUDENT'S TYPO

He wasn't surprised. What town wasn't?
Everywhere the mists of property, the mists
of language. Every Main Street he'd known
shrouded in itself. The mist-filled churches
and the mist-filled stores in strange collusion.

Nevertheless, this was where he chose to live.
Clarities, after all, were supposed to be hidden;
otherwise, no fun in the classroom or in the field.
Life? His neighbors preferred the movie versions,
loose ends tied up, mists of romance and thrill.
And sometimes he did, too.

Now and again he'd get underneath, see
snakes in among the flowers, hearts askew.
And friends from cities would report
they'd been places where the mists had risen.
You needed to look aslant, they said,
so dangerous would the real appear at first.

No safety in the universe. He'd stay put.
Besides, he liked to be in the mists of tall trees
and in the mists of what made him hungry for more.
He liked the mistiness of familiar boundaries
so he could let in, secretly, what he loved.

And the chaos? It favored no geography,
a perpetual rumbling beneath and above him
wherever he was. He had lived with it so long
it was simply the music he worked to, slept to
and woke with, in the mists of all.

ANOTHER MAN

In the Atlantic City bus station, well past dawn,
  the good light illuminates
a few off-duty whores, while a no-man's man

with dreadlocks hawks crack in a corner
  near the men's room.
And here's the rest of us, blackjack crazies

and slot queens, all-nighters, eyes deeply circled,
  and me, ready to play
Virgil to a friend bussing in to test his luck.

The man seated in front of me, not wanting
  anyone to miss his beauty,
has taken off his shirt in this December cool.

He stands, turns. Waist to neck
  he's one large tattoo.
With each move three mermaids

and a ball of snakes move too, his skin
  an intricate, pulsing blue.
I imagine someone running her fingers

over him and his art, even pressing her lips
  to it, astounded
such a wild, rare animal could be loose,

someone he might have found and lost
  among the dreary repetitions
of this gambling town. He turns again

as if he were thinking: If only she could see
  my anchor, my new skull
& bones, my arrow-pierced heart.

My friend arrives, dressed in black—
  his mojo, he calls it,
his anti-Trump. He has money to burn

and thinks I know how to skirt the fires.
  I shake his hand
and lead him toward where I've often become

another man for a while, masked
  now with hope
for his sake, sage of the slim chance.

MEN IN THE SKY

Leaves are falling as the telephone men
ascend to the tops of poles.
They are riding a magic long-armed
machine. No need anymore to climb.
To speak through wires is as natural now
as falling leaves, natural as men in the sky.
The telephone men in the cupped palm
of the long arm are reducing the static,
helping me reach far out of town.
They are beautiful in their hard orange
plumage. Finches and cardinals: mere birds
by comparison, unchangeable, nervous.
It's a shame the men must come down.
I stood next to them at the 7-Eleven
at lunch break, heard them order ham
and cheese on a hard roll, Dr Pepper.
I saw them get out of their trucks
and spit. Now the leaves graze
their shoulders suddenly more golden
for having touched them. My phone
is ringing. It's one of the telephone men,
the highest, the one with a sufficiency
of tools around his waist, calling to see
if everything's all right. Everything isn't.

EMPERORS

On my ripped, screened-in porch,
the black flies had at me, no fault
but mine. Of all things in the world
unfixable, that screen wasn't one.
I was the emperor of in-between,
of perhaps, of someday soon.
The newspaper said war. This time
its funnies weren't funny enough
to show us who we were.
My favorite second baseman
had gone 0 for 5—there it was,
in black and white. How many of us
could bear a daily record
of exactly what we'd done?
Dark clouds moved in
from the west. The wind hid itself
in the pitch pines and oaks,
always invisible when still.
Mendacity and love, high spirits
and gloom—nothing was new.
Somewhere in between
we tried our best.
The dog huddled by my legs
anticipating the storm.

From her window a mother summoned
her child who yelled "No"
and then "Please." And though
he knew what was coming,
or maybe *because* he knew,
the emperor across the street
kept mowing his lawn.

ONE MOMENT AND THE NEXT
IN THE PINE BARRENS

One moment a crow
on the highway's white line
is eating a dead thing,
the next a falling pinecone
leads my eye to a lost wallet.
I tell my wife
I think I'm in a story
the world is making for me.
In it I'm merely a bit player,
a walk-on. I'm saddened
when she doesn't disagree.
The wallet has $80 in it,
a slew of credit cards.
Hungry for praise
more than anything else,
I know I'll return it intact.
One moment a possum or
groundhog or small gray thing
allows itself to be frightened by us,
the next we see a trail
through the woods
marked with white thumbtacks.
Someone has placed them

eye-level on the tree trunks,
and we follow them
to an old wooden bridge
over a brook. My wife says,
We're living in a kind
of story where much is promised
and little happens,
the kind of story a fancy writer
might call "The Conundrums
of the Palpable,"
believing that could save it.
I don't disagree.
One moment mysterious thumbtacks,
next I'm standing on a bridge,
a tourist in the comedy
thoroughly lost with a clear view.

AFTERLIFE

There've been times I've thought worms
  might be beneficent, speeding up,
as they do, the dissolution of the body,

I've imagined myself streamlined, all bone
  and severity,
pure mind, free to contemplate the startling

absence of any useful metaphysics, any final
  punishment or reward.
Indulgences, no doubt. Romances I've allowed myself

when nothing ached, and the long diminishment
  seemed far off.
Today I want my body to keep making its sloppy

requests. I'm out among the wayward dazzle
  of the countryside,
which is its own afterlife, wild, repeatable.

There's no lesson in it for me. I just like
  its ignorant thrust,
it's sure way back, after months without desire.

Are wildflowers holy? Are weeds?
  There's infinite hope
if both are, but perphaps not for us.

To skirt the woods, to walk deeply like this
  into the high grass,
is to invoke the phantasms of sense

and importance. I think I'm smelling the rain
  we can smell before it rains.
It's the odor of another world, I'm convinced,

and means nothing, yet here it is, and here
  sweetly it comes
from the gray sky into the small openings.

CHOKECHERRY

Early fog, the morning almost invisible.
Skink is a lizard. Chalcedony a stone.
There's refuge in nouns.

Deep Gap. Burnt Cabins—the names of towns.
Jack-in-the-pulpit. Sweet William—plants,
and nightshade one that can kill.

Bobwhite and whippoorwill insist on themselves.
The mockingbird indiscriminately collects.
Narcissist: a flower of a man.

One tries hard to reduce a night's aftertaste,
a querulous heart.
Chokecherry is a gorgeous, bitter fruit.

This fine-grained agate on the desk,
this paperweight, once kept
better company with slugs and worms.

Whoever named the birds with bad names—
Cock-of-the-rock, shrike, sapsucker—
must have wanted to make something clear.

NATURE

Spring's hesitant splendor had given way
to steady rains. The sky kept crumbling
and the laurels whitened and everywhere
a ripeness was visible. Nature was okay.
For me it had its place, scaffolding and
backdrop to the stage on which people
ruined and saved themselves, played out
who they were. I liked its animals best,
the big cats and the preposterous mad-God
creations like tapirs or rhinoceri.
A rose, well, a rose was
just a prom queen standing still
for a photo. Mountain sunsets,
waterfalls, they were postcards to send
to good friends who trusted happiness
occurred, if at all, in other places.
It had rained now for so many days
rain had become another form of silence.
Granted there was beauty to it as well,
gray against gray. If you stared long enough:
tiny shadings, as if someone had painted
the varieties of boredom.
And the rain made puddles on the tennis courts,
spoiling one of my pleasures.

It made some of us contemplative, soul-searching,
who had lives that couldn't bear scrutiny.
Summer was upon us. I could only hope
that it might contain enough contraries
to make it a season of plenty.
Soon I'd seek out someone not sad
to whom weather or beauty was a pretense
to get together, and drive to Cape May Point
where marshland and dune converge.
Last fall, there on the nature trail
in early morning fog, a lone man disappeared
and reappeared, in and out, until the fog
seemed to dissolve him, color him its own.
Gray, then, was the only truth in the world.

BURYING THE CAT

Her name was Isadora and, like all cats,
she was a machine made of rubber bands
and muscle, exemplar of crouch
and pounce, genius of leisure. Seventeen years old.
A neighbor dog had broken her back,
and the owner called when he saw my car
pull into the driveway. He'd put her
in a plastic sack. It was ridiculous
how heavy she was, how inflexible.
For years I've known that to confess
is to say what one doesn't feel. I hereby
confess I was not angry with that dog,
a shepherd, who had seen something foreign
on his property. I'd like to say I was feeling
a sadness so numb that I was a machine myself,
with bad cogs and faulty wiring. But
I'm telling this three years after the fact.
Nothing is quite what it was
after we've formed a clear picture of it.
Behind our house there's a field, a half-acre
of grass good for the sailing of a Frisbee.
I buried her there. My thought was to do it

before the children came home from school,
my wife from work. I got the shovel
from the shed. The ground was not without
resistance. I put several stones on top,
pyramid style, a crude mausoleum. What
we're mostly faced with are these privacies,
inconsequential to all but us. But I wasn't
thinking that then. I kicked some dirt
off the shovel, returned it to the shed.
I remember feeling that strange satisfaction
I'd often felt after yardwork, some evidence
of what I'd done visible for a change.
I remember that after their shock, their grief,
I expected to be praised.

OKLAHOMA CITY

The accused chose to plead innocent
because he was guilty. We allowed such a thing;
it was one of our greatnesses, nutty, protective.
On the car radio a survivor's ordeal, her leg
amputated without anesthesia while trapped

under a steel girder. Simply, no big words—
that's how people tell their horror stories.
I was elsewhere, on my way to a party.
On arrival, everyone was sure to be carrying
a piece of the awful world with him.

Not one of us wouldn't be smiling.
There'd be drinks, irony, hidden animosities.
Something large would be missing.
But most of us would understand
something large always would be missing.

Oklahoma City was America reduced
to McVeigh's half-thought-out thoughts.
Did he know anything about suffering?
It's the naïve among us who are guilty
of wondering if we're moral agents or madmen

or merely, as one scientist said,
a fortuitous collocation of atoms.
Some mysteries can be solved by ampersands.
*And*s not *or*s; that was my latest answer.
At the party two women were talking

about how strange it is that they still like men.
They were young and unavailable, and their lovely faces
evoked a world not wholly incongruent
with the world I know. I had no illusions, not even hopes,
that their beauty had anything to do with goodness.

BACKWATERS

My dogs were dead and it was winter;
I had no good reason to walk the beach
in Brigantine, as if reasons mattered.
Aren't they what we manufacture?
The sea was whitecap and wind, the gulls loners
standing in groups, mild practitioners of avarice.
I knew them well. Driftwood, as ever,
vaguely resembled something intentional.
For months now, crazed high school kids
and postal clerks had been revealing
what exists in the odd backwaters of their hearts.
I'm sorry, I said to myself without apology,
but it's all much worse than it's ever been.
Brigantine—I heard prison and freedom
in that name. Walking a beach so called
felt appropriately in between. In proper time
the cold, like conscience, urged me home,
and I sought the calm on the lee side
of the dunes. A used condom, two empty
beer cans, lay in the indented sand.
Even in winter, I thought, for a moment pleased,
then felt in the presence of trash.

I looked seaward, forced myself back
out into the bracing wind.
There at the end of a crude jetty made of rocks
a hooded man was staring into the monotony.
You don't speak to a man like that.
You give him all the room he needs.

PHANTOM

It's the last hour of a final day
in June, my wife sleeping,
Bob Dylan going ninety miles an hour
down a dead-end street,
and moments ago—bless the mind
that works against itself—
Hegel conceding that philosophy
always arrives too late.
Through his cat door
here comes our orange cat,
empty-mouthed, looking bereft.
Voles and mice, don't dare relax.
Loners and dreamers, time to test
the dark, visit the haunts.
I'm waiting for that click
of the tape deck or the chapter's end,
whichever comes first—one of those
deals you make with yourself.
It's the click. Now I'll take to bed
this body and the phantom
of what it once was, inseparable

as they are these days, smoke
rising from a stubborn fire.
Night light, be my guide.
I can feel my way just so far.

A POSTMORTEM GUIDE

For my eulogist, in advance

Do not praise me for my exceptional serenity.
Can't you see I've turned away
from the large excitements,
and have accepted all the troubles?

Go down to the old cemetery; you'll see
there's nothing definitive to be said.
The dead once were all kinds—
boundary breakers and scalawags,
martyrs of the flesh, and so many
dumb bunnies of duty, unbearably nice.

I've been a little of each.

And, please, resist the temptation
of speaking about virtue.
The seldom-tempted are too fond
of that word, the small-
spirited, the unburdened.
Know that I've admired in others
only the fraught straining
to be good.

Adam's my man and Eve's not to blame.
He bit in; it made no sense to stop.

Still, for accuracy's sake you might say
I often stopped,
that I rarely went as far as I dreamed.

And since you know my hardships,
understand they're mere bump and setback
against history's horror.
Remind those seated, perhaps weeping,
how obscene it is
for some of us to complain.

Tell them I had second chances.
I knew joy.
I was burned by books early
and kept sidling up to the flame.

Tell them that at the end I had no need
for God, who'd become just a story
I once loved, one of many
with concealments and late-night rescues,
high sentence and pomp. The truth is

I learned to live without hope
as well as I could, almost happily,
in the despoiled and radiant now.

You who are one of them, say that I loved
my companions most of all.
In all sincerity, say that they provided
a better way to be alone.